Before you start ...

1 Gather together everything you need for the activity using the equipment list at the top of each page. Collect lots of different materials, from seashells to bottle tops, that you can use for making things.

2 Cover your worktable with newspaper and wear an apron to protect your clothes.

3 Read all the instructions carefully. Always wait for glue and paint to dry.

4 Be very careful with scissors and knives. Only use them if an adult is there to help you.

5 When you have finished an activity, wash your hands and put everything away.

DK

A DK PUBLISHING BOOK

Written and edited by Dawn Sirett and Lara Tankel
Art Editors Mandy Earey and Mary Sandberg
Additional design Veneta Altham
Deputy Managing Art Editor C. David Gillingwater
US Editor Camela Decaire
Production Fiona Baxter
Dib, Dab, and Dob made by Wilfrid Wood
Photography by Alex Wilson and Norman Hollands
Illustrations by Peter Kavanagh
Spoon puppets, fish, and monster made by Jane Bull

First American Edition, 1997
2 4 6 8 10 9 7 5 3 1

Published in the United States by DK Publishing, Inc.
95 Madison Avenue, New York, New York 10016

Copyright © 1997 Dorling Kindersley Limited, London
Visit us on the World Wide Web at http://www.dk.com

Published in Great Britain by Dorling Kindersley Ltd.

A CIP catalog record for this book is
available from the Library of Congress.

ISBN 0-7894-1522-4

Color reproduction by Colourscan, Singapore
Printed and bound in Hong Kong by Imago

PLAY AND LEARN
Making Things

With Dib, Dab, and Dob

paint paintbrush wooden spoon poster board scissors

Turn spoons into puppets

Paint a design on a wooden spoon.

Cut legs or ears from poster board and glue them on.

Glue on pipe cleaners or yarn for hair, horns, or antennae.

scissors colored cord dried pasta tubes

Turn pasta into jewelry

Cut a length of cord a little longer than you want your necklace to be.

I've tied a knot in one end of the cord to stop the pasta from falling off.

Thread pasta tubes onto the cord.

Finally, tie the
ends together
to make a
necklace.

I've used
beads and made a
bracelet, too.

large sheets of tissue paper felt-tip pens scissors white glue

Make a flying fish

Fold a square of tissue paper in half. Draw a fish on the paper with a big mouth and tail.

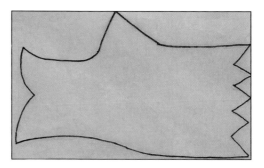

Cut out the fish. Glue the long sides together, leaving the tail and mouth open.

clear tape   hole punch thin yarn

Decorate each side of the fish.

It's almost finished now, Dib.

Stick tape on the corners of the mouth on both sides of the fish. Punch holes through the taped corners.

Up, up, and away!

Thread the ends of a long length of yarn through the holes you have made. Tie a knot in each one.

The tape will stop the holes from tearing.

Try making other designs. A rocket works well.

The quicker I run, the higher they fly!

To make your fish fly, hold the yarn and run around quickly.

rice · two plastic cups · masking tape · white glue · buttons

Make noisy shakers

Pour some rice into a plastic cup.

That should be enough.

Turn another cup upside down and tape it to the first cup.

scissors  cardboard yarn white glue fake toy eyes

Wind yarn to make a pom-pom

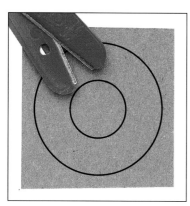

Ask an adult to cut out two cardboard rings. The rings need to be the same size.

Hold the rings together and wind lengths of yarn around them. When you reach the end of a length, knot it to a new one and keep winding.

Wind the yarn through the hole and around the ring.

felt

pipe cleaners

Stop when you can't wind on any more yarn. Then ask an adult to cut through the yarn, as shown.

Cut through the yarn around the edge of the rings.

Then wrap a long length of yarn between the two rings and tie a tight knot. Pull off the rings.

Pom-pom party

Glue on toy eyes, felt, and
pipe cleaners to transform
your pom-pom into a pet.

Try threading pom-poms together to make a hairy caterpillar.

What kind of pet are you going to make?

Make a garbage monster

Find some empty boxes that you can use to make a monster. Paint them and leave them to dry.

Then glue the boxes together to make a monster shape.